ISBN: 9798674977803

In loving memory of Brian and Veronica
Whose love and encouragement was endless
xxx

Acknowledgements

Having spent nearly twenty years working with children and young people, books and stories have played a huge part in all aspects of my career. From sharing stories in nurseries, to researching lessons as a lecturer, to studying the way that books are created in my degree. Books are such special things, they have a magical ability to allow us to lose ourselves in their pages, to feel like we are at one with the characters and find resolution in their storylines. My love of books has been one which spans years, and some of my favourites still sit on my book shelf. In 2014 I left my full-time teaching post and told my tutor group that I would dedicate my time to developing my book collection, which had sat as an idea in notebooks for so long. On the arrival of Brian, my real-life cockapoo, in 2015 the dream just became more and more real. I am delighted to be able to share the Adventures of Brian with families and bring the magic of books and the wonders of therapeutic storytelling together to offer a combination of stories and support to children. Before we start this special story, there is thanks to be given;

To my Mum and Dad, who have given me the encouragement to move forward with a dream of creating stories to help small people. Thank you for standing by me, encouraging me and sharing these precious moments.

To Richard for your belief and encouragement that there was a set of books inside me that should be written, this shiny diamond is very grateful.

To my nan and grandad, who forever guide me to follow this path that I am on and to ensure that I stay true to my dreams.

To Veronica and Brian, eternally in my heart, you inspired the little fluffy boy who became the centre of these books and shared so many precious memories.

Finally, to all our friends who have supported us, encouraged us and inspired us in the development of the Adventures of Brian, we are so grateful for your love each and every day.

I hope you enjoy these books as much as I have enjoyed writing them

Love Nicky x x

THE ADVENTURES OF BRIAN

This book belongs to:

....

Brian wandered around the house with the funny feeling in his tummy. He just could not sit still. No matter what he did, the funny feeling in his tummy would not disappear.

Brian wandered into the garden and looked at his ball, but the funny feeling hurt his tummy, so instead of playing he flopped on the grass.

At that moment, Blue Butterfly was floating past. When she saw Brian's sad face she floated down onto the flower next to him.

"Brian, what is the matter?" she asked gently.

Brian looked up at his best friend and started to cry. He cried, and cried and cried. Brian wondered if the tears would ever stop.

When the tears finally slowed down, Brian looked up at Blue Butterfly and replied, "I start school soon and I am ever so scared!" then he started to cry again.

Blue Butterfly let Brian let all his feelings out, and as he calmed down she softly whispered, "do you want to tell me what is scaring you Brian?".

Brian took a big breath and nodded very slowly. He began wandering around the garden again, before starting to tell Blue Butterfly all his worries. "I'm scared that I won't make any friends" he whispered to Blue Butterfly.

Blue Butterfly nodded.

"I'm scared that I will get lost, my school seems very big!" Brian said, a little bit louder.

Blue Butterfly nodded again.

"Most of all, I am scared that I will miss my mummy!" Brian told her, as a big tear rolled down his fur.

Blue Butterfly listened, Brian thought it was very helpful that she listened so carefully to him. After a little while, she said,

"I can understand why you are scared Brian, new things can make us worry about what will happen next".

Brian thought about this, new things did make him worry, because he did not know what to expect. Blue Butterfly always understood.

Blue Butterfly fluttered her wings and settled down on her flower, looking at Brian closely. Brian waited to see what she would say.

"Brian, going to school is very exciting, and there are lots of things you can do to make your worries feel better" she told him.

Brian's ears twitched, this made him much more excited, he really did, want to go to school. "What can I do?" he asked.

Blue Butterfly nodded, "Well Brian, when you want to make friends, it is important to be kind to others, make sure you smile, and you could invite them to play with you" she said. Brian thought about this, "what if they don't want to play with me?" he asked.

Blue Butterfly smiled. Well, Brian thought she smiled, it was hard to tell. "Brian, sometimes people will not want to play, but you can ask others. You can also check to see if there are some children who are on their own. They might be too shy or unsure to ask, so if you ask them they might want to play too."

Brian realised that Blue Butterfly was right. Sometimes, he felt too shy to ask people to play, so he stood alone. If he asked the children to play, they might like to play with him.

"What about if I get lost?" Brian asked. Blue Butterfly nodded again, "When you start school, your teachers will help you to find your classroom, and where to go. You just need to make sure you listen carefully" she told him.

Brian looked at her as he thought, this made sense. "What about at lunch time?' he asked.

Blue Butterfly fluttered her wings, "at lunch time, you can ask the teachers and lunch supervisors, they are there to help you, and to show you what to do?" she told him.

Brian felt better about this, "so, there are lots of people to help me?" he asked.

"There are lots of people to help you Brian, just make sure you listen to their instructions, and the more you go to school the easier it will be to remember" Blue Butterfly told him.

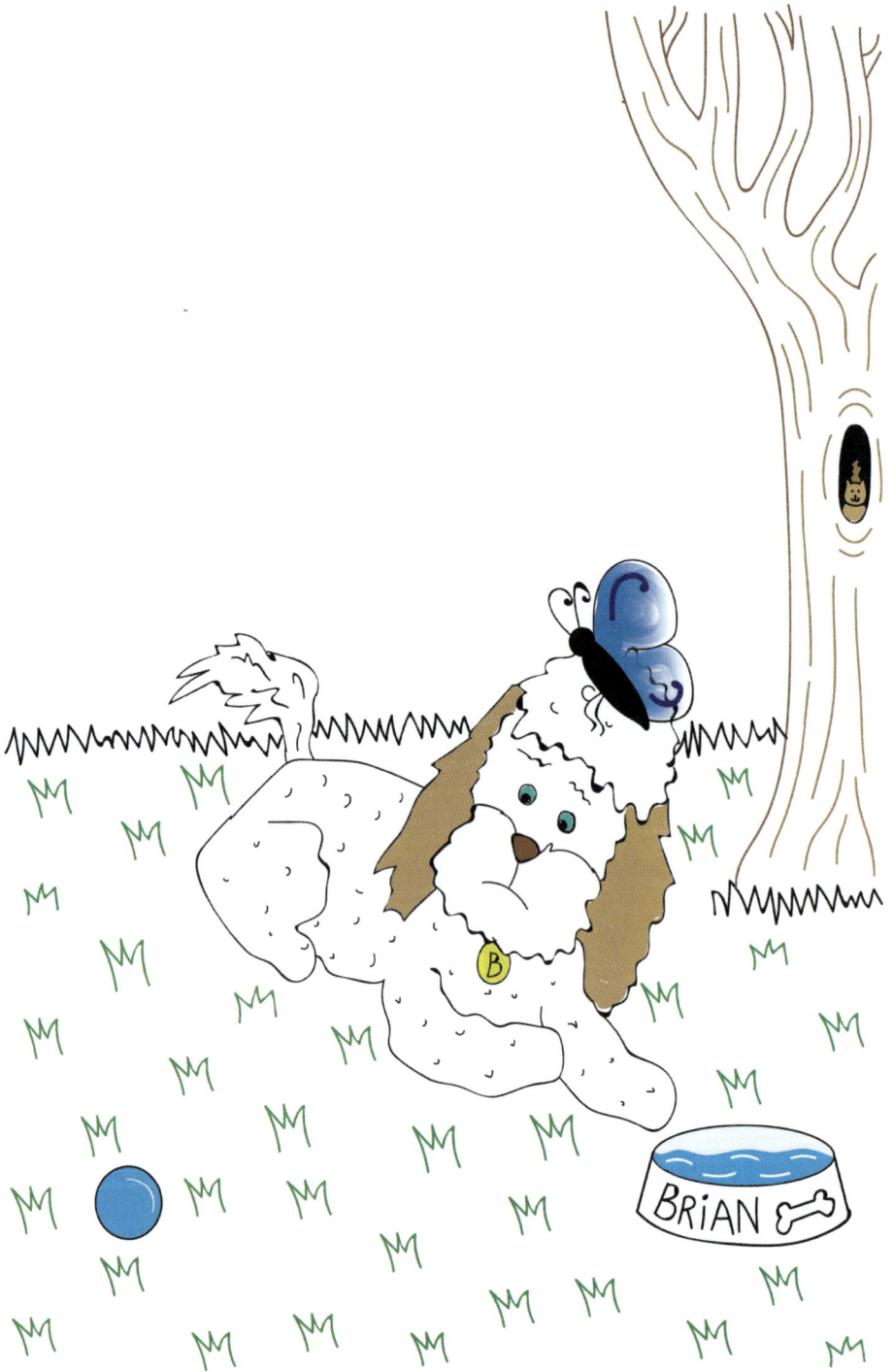

Brian realised that Blue Butterfly was right, the more that he went to school, the easier it would be. He just needed to practice. He noticed that the feeling in his tummy was getting better now that he had told someone his worries.

He remembered that there was one more worry that needed some help though, "I'm really going to miss my mummy" Brian whispered.

Blue Butterfly fluttered onto Brain's head and fluffed his hair, Brian thought it was a butterfly hug.

"It's ok to miss the people we love Brian" she told him. "Your mummy will be there to pick you up at home time, and sometimes even nanny and grandad might pick you up too!" she told him.

Brian's ears twitched, he had not realised that nanny and grandad might collect him, that might be lots of fun!

"It can be a good plan to take something to remind you of your mummy with you" Blue Butterfly suggested.

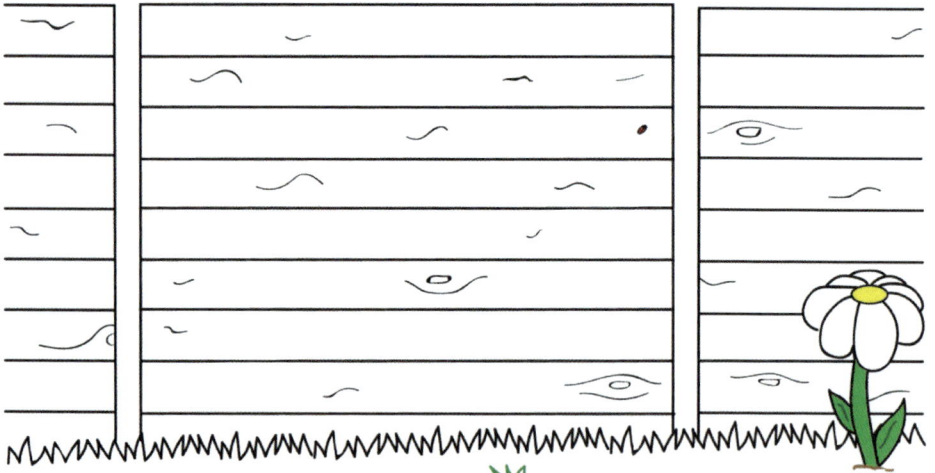

Brian thought about this, it would help if he could take something that reminded him of his mummy.

"What could I take with me?" he asked Blue Butterfly.

Blue Butterfly floated back onto her flower. "It's best that it is something small that will not get lost" she told him.

Brian thought, what did he have that was small?

Blue Butterfly already had an idea…. "You might like to make a key ring with a picture of you and your mummy to put on your lunch bag" she suggested.

Brian thought about this, a keyring would mean he had his mummy's picture, and he could look at it at lunch time then, that would make him feel better.

"Blue Butterfly, that is a great idea!" he told her, wagging his tail and smiling with excitement.

Blue Butterfly felt very happy that she could help. She looked at Brian's wagging tail and smiled to herself, it was good to help people find ways to feel better.

Brian grinned at Blue Butterfly, he realised that his funny feelings were nearly all gone, talking to her had really helped. "I already feel better!" he told her.

"That makes me feel really happy", Blue Butterfly told him, "you need to get your things ready, but I will come and find out about school soon!" she told him as she floated into the sky.

The next day, Brian woke up full of excitement to make his key ring and get his things ready for school. He bounced down the stairs and found his mummy with her keys in her hand.

Brian's tail started to wiggle. He always knew there was an adventure in store when he saw the keys. "Would you like to go and visit your school?" his mummy asked.

Welcome!

abcdefghijklm

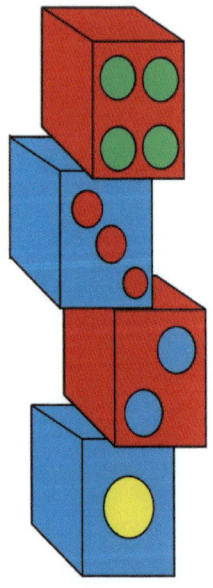

Brian grinned, a visit would really help him to start to learn where things are. He leapt up and kissed his mummy and ran out the door with her.

As Brian wandered around his school, he looked at all the walls, the rooms and the corridors. It was big, but he realised that it was quite simple to find things if he followed the carpet path through the school. There were also lots of people he could ask.

Brian's funny feelings were getting smaller and smaller. He felt much better after he had seen everything, he really loved the playground, and everyone was very smiley. His mummy took some photos so that they could look at them at home.

When they got home, Brian was keen to make his keyring.

His mummy had brought him an empty keyring and they looked at the photographs together to find one that he liked. Brian smiled as he looked at all the photographs, there were lots of happy memories.

Very carefully, his mummy helped to cut out the picture so that it would fit inside the keyring. Once it was inside, they clipped the keyring together and Brian grinned.

He helped his mummy to clip it to his lunch bag, so that each lunch time he would be able to look at the picture.

Brian knew that his mummy would be there to pick him up at home time. He knew that if he looked at his keyring at lunch time, it was half way through his day and half way to seeing mummy again for cuddles.

Welcome!

a b c d e f g h i j k l m

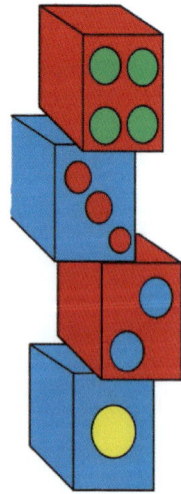

The next morning, it was time for Brian's first day at school. Brian woke up with butterflies and funny feelings in his tummy. He was a little bit scared and a little bit excited, it felt like his tummy was dancing!

He bounced downstairs, and his mummy made him breakfast and gave him a hug. After some breakfast and a drink, his tummy felt a bit better. Brian knew that the feelings would get better once he met everyone.

On the walk to school, Brian looked all around him, he saw everyone else walking to school too.

At the school door, his teacher was ready to greet him with a big smile. His mummy helped him to hang up his school things so that Brian knew where they were. Brian gave his mummy a big hug and a kiss, she pointed at where she would be to pick him up. Brian nodded, he knew where to look when they went home now.

He took a big breath and wandered into his classroom.

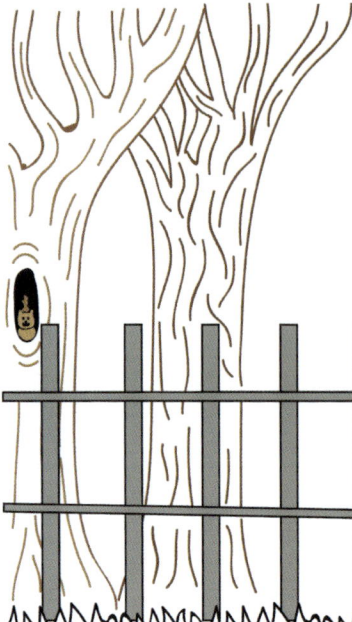

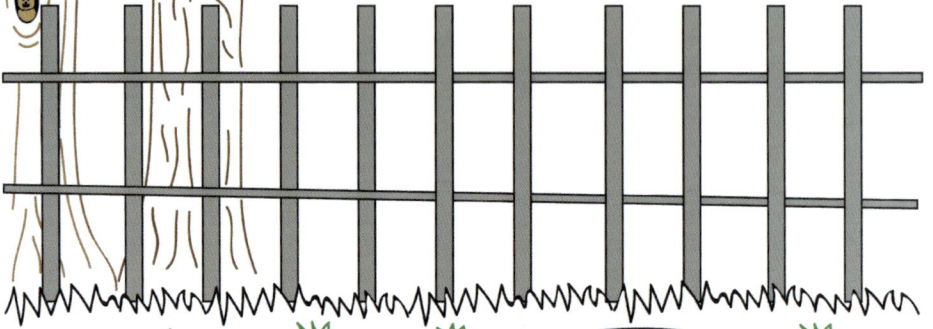

Brian found, that as the day went by, it got easier and easier. His teacher gave lots of instructions to help him and he made sure he listened very carefully. He realised that everyone was a little bit nervous, so they all helped each other.

At lunch time, he sat with his lunch bag, looked at his key ring and smiled, he knew it was half way until he saw his mummy and could tell her all the good things he had found out about school.

At break time, Brian remembered to smile, and asked others from his class if he could play, they had lots of fun together.

Brian realised that Blue Butterfly had been right, school was exciting. He had lots to do and when his teacher said it was home time he was so happy to see his mummy!

Brian ran out the door, and there was his mummy, waiting for him, just like she promised!

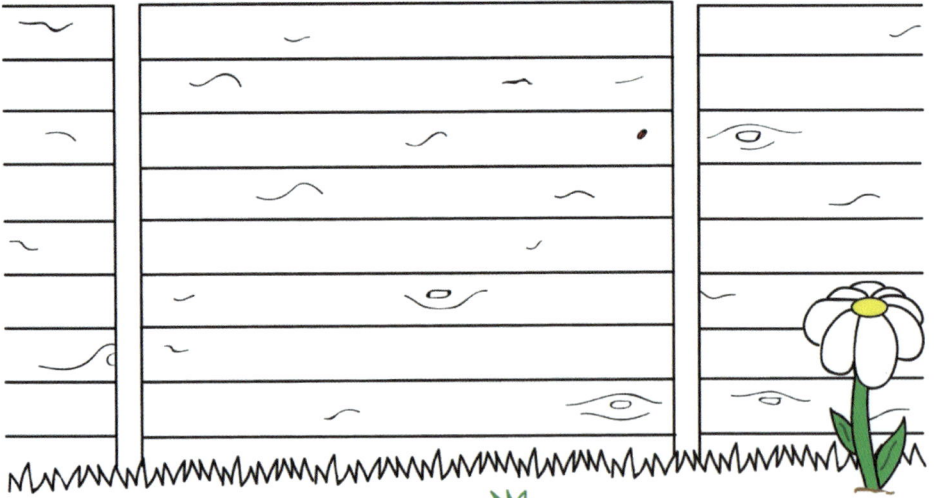

Every day that Brian went to school, he learned more and more.

Each day that he went to school he felt more and more comfortable.

With every day that he went to school, Brian made more friends.

Every day that he finished, his mummy was stood waiting for him in the playground, just like she promised.

Brian loved coming home and sitting in the garden to tell Blue Butterfly about the new things he had learnt, and to tell her about the memories he made. Blue Butterfly told him that she was very proud of him.

Brian felt proud of himself too, he realised that school was lots of fun!

THE ADVENTURES OF BRIAN

HELPING CHILDREN OVERCOME THEIR FEARS AND WORRIES

Other books in this series:

Brian and the Blue Butterfly

Brian and the Magic Night

Brian and the Black Pebble

Brian and the Christmas Wish

Brian and the Shiny Star

Brian and the Naughty Day

Brian and the Funny Feeling

Brian and the Poorly Day

Brian and the Big Black Dog

Brian and the Scary Moment

Brian and the Proud Feeling

Brian and the Sparkly Rainbow

Brian and Boo's Big Adventure (Special Edition)

Brian and the Changing Path

Brian and the Christmas Sparkle

Brian and the Night-time Noise

Brian and the Rescue Pups

Brian and the Forever Family (Special Edition)

Brian and the Troubling Thoughts

Brian and the Kind Deeds

Brian and the Christmas Box

Brian and the Honey Bees

Brian and the Shaky Paws

Brian and the New School

Nicky lives in Sussex with Brian the Cockapoo where they enjoy daily adventures with friends and family. Nicky started her career by spending 10 years working in the early years sector with 0-5 year olds before lecturing in early years and health and social care to students aged 16 and over. She later retrained as a hypnotherapist and now runs A Step at a Time Hypnotherapy working with children and adults to resolve their personal issues.

The Adventures of Brian books were the development of a dream of wanting to offer parents of young children tools and resources to support their children to manage worries and fears in a non-intrusive way. Having spent a large part of her career reading stories at all speeds and in all voices this collection of storybooks was born.

Each book in the collection covers a different worry which affects children on a day to day basis and uses therapeutic storytelling to support children in resolving these through Brian's daily adventures.

You can find more titles in the Adventures of Brian series by visiting:

www.adventuresofbrian.co.uk

Printed in Great Britain
by Amazon